Scales and Tails

Meet the Iguana

Suzanne Buckingham

PowerKiDS press.

New York

To my very special friends, Molly and Colin Bath

Published in 2009 by The Rosen Publishing Group, Inc.
29 East 21st Street, New York, NY 10010

First Edition

Editor: Joanne Randolph
Book Design: Greg Tucker
Photo Researcher: Jessica Gerweck

Photo Credits: Back cover, cover (logo), cover, pp. 1, 6, 9, 12–13, 15, 19 Shutterstock.com; p. 10 © Biosphoto/Delfino Dominique/Peter Arnold, Inc.; p. 16 © age fotostock/Superstock; p. 20 © Getty Images.

Library of Congress Cataloging-in-Publication Data

Buckingham, Suzanne.
  Meet the iguana / Suzanne Buckingham. — 1st ed.
      p. cm. — (Scales and tails)
  Includes index.
  ISBN 978-1-4042-4499-3 (library binding)
  1. Iguana (Genus)—Juvenile literature. I. Title.
  QL666.L25B83 2009
  597.95'42—dc22

                                2008002879

Manufactured in the United States of America

Contents

Meet the Scaly Iguana

What animal has a long tail, tiny scales all over its body, and sharp claws on its feet? This crawling animal is an iguana! Iguanas are lizards. Most iguanas are green, but some are blue, brown, and gray.

Like you, iguanas sleep at night and are awake during the day. In the daytime they hunt for food and **bask** in the hot sun. Iguanas are cold blooded. This means their bodies cannot make heat, so they live in warm places. Iguanas have been around for thousands of years. Let's learn more about this **ancient** lizard!

This green iguana basks in the sun. Even though this is a green iguana, you can see that its scales have many different colors.

Marine iguanas, like this one, are water lovers. They swim in the ocean to find food.

So Many Iguanas

There are about 700 different kinds of iguanas in the world. Iguanas are found in many different **habitats**, such as deserts, islands, and rain forests. Desert iguanas live in Arizona, California, and New Mexico. They are brown with white spots. These small iguanas are only 10 to 16 inches (25–41 cm) long.

Marine iguanas live near the **equator** on the Galápagos Islands. Marine iguanas are about 5 feet (1.5 m) long. Green iguanas live in the rain forests of Mexico, Central America, and South America. These giants grow up to 7 feet (2 m) long.

Iguana Homes

Iguanas have many different kinds of homes. Desert iguanas live under shady bushes during the hottest part of the day. At night, desert iguanas crawl into underground **burrows**, where the earth keeps them warm.

After walking on the beach or swimming during the day, marine iguanas stay on rocks near the shore at night. There the iguanas lie on top of each other to stay warm.

Green iguanas make their homes high up in the treetops of the rain forest. They often sit on branches over ponds or rivers. Sometimes green iguanas leave the trees to sun themselves on rocks.

This iguana makes its home in the dry, sandy desert. It has climbed up a pointy cactus to look for food or a spot to sun itself.

This land iguana eats a cactus on one of the Galápagos Islands. The iguana uses its feet to get rid of large thorns from the cactus, eating the rest.

Time to Eat

Most iguanas are **herbivores**, so they eat only plants, but some eat meat. Desert iguanas generally feast on fruit, flowers, grasses, bushes, and cacti. They are also known to eat bugs and dead animals if they find them.

Seaweed is the chief food of marine iguanas. Young iguanas and their mothers eat seaweed in the waters close to shore. Strong males will swim up to 60 feet (18 m) under water to find their leafy meals.

Green iguanas dine on fruit, berries, leaves, and flower buds they find in the rain forest. Some green iguanas also eat mice, birds, and bird eggs.

The Iguana

Scaly Facts

- A marine iguana's body takes in too much salt while it is diving for seaweed. The iguana gets rid of the extra salt by blowing it out through its nose!

- Iguanas often change color if they get hot or cold. When it is cold, they get darker. In the hot sunlight, they get lighter.

- Like humans, iguanas have five toes on their feet. The sharp claws on the ends of their toes help them climb rocks and trees.

- In South America, green iguanas are often called chicken of the trees. The people there like to eat iguanas and say their meat tastes like chicken!

- Marine iguanas can swim underwater for 15 minutes without coming up for air!

- Male green iguanas have pieces of skin called dewlaps, which hang under their chins. They puff out their dewlaps to scare off enemies.

What a Tail!

An iguana's tail can grow up to three times the length of its body. Iguanas use their long tails for balance. These strong tails also help iguanas swim.

Most iguanas use their tails to stay safe. For example, green iguanas will scare off enemies by hitting them with their tails. Their powerful tails are strong enough to break the bones of small animals. If an enemy catches a green iguana by its tail, the tail will break off so the iguana can get away. A new tail will grow back in a few weeks.

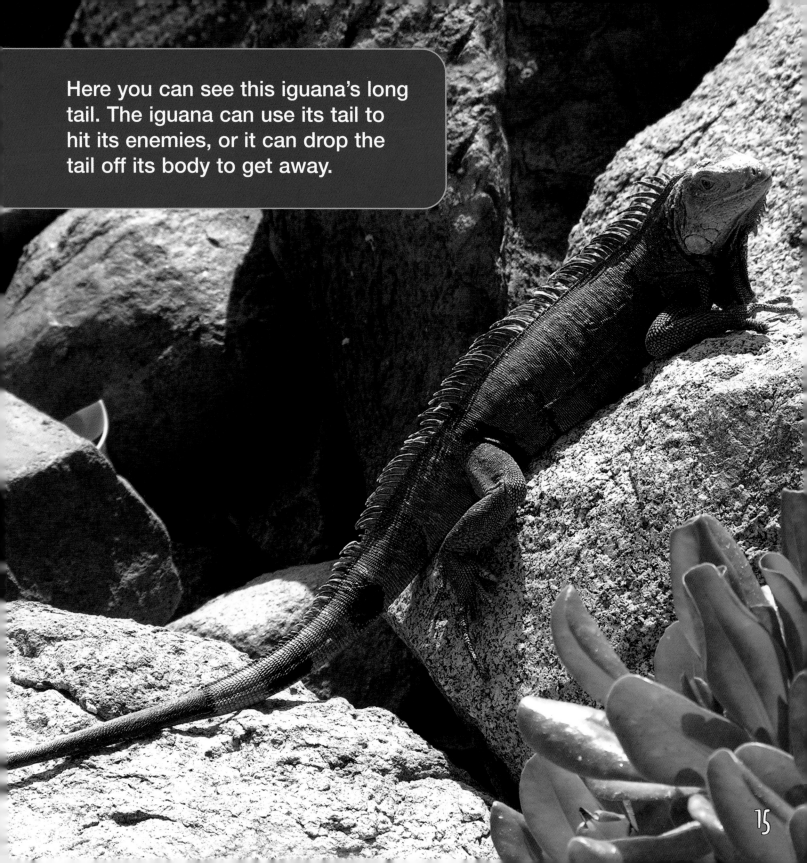

Here you can see this iguana's long tail. The iguana can use its tail to hit its enemies, or it can drop the tail off its body to get away.

Here a green iguana breaks free from its egg.
A baby iguana looks just like its mother and
father when it is born, only smaller.

Out of My Shell

An iguana begins its life inside a tiny egg. Mother iguanas dig small burrows for their eggs. They lay about 20 to 40 eggs at one time. After covering their eggs with soil, warm sunlight heats the soil and **incubates** the eggs. After 65 to 115 days, depending on the type of iguana, new babies **hatch**.

Young iguanas must hide from their enemies to stay safe. They also need to find their own food. As they grow larger, iguanas shed their tight outer skin several times. An iguana becomes an adult around the age of two or three.

On Its Own

All the eggs in an iguana **clutch** hatch at about the same time. Newborn iguana babies are called hatchlings. After a hatchling crawls from its egg, it must dig out of the burrow.

A hatchling has to take care of itself because its parents are not around. A hungry baby iguana must search for its own food. It looks for meals of insects or tasty plants. Tiny hatchlings cannot move fast, so it is easy for snakes, birds, and other **predators** to catch them. People also hunt hatchlings to sell for pets. With so many dangers, few hatchlings grow into adults.

This iguana sheds its skin as it grows larger. Young iguanas shed their skin more often than adult ones.

This boy spends some time with a pet iguana. Iguanas are not easy pets to own, but many people find the hard work is worth it.

Iguanas in Your House

The most liked **reptile** pet in the United States is the green iguana. Iguana owners must take good care of their scaly pets so they will live long, healthy lives.

Iguanas require plenty of fresh drinking water. They like to eat green, leafy vegetables, such as dandelion greens and spinach. Iguanas bask in the sun in their natural habitat to stay warm so they need special warming lights in their cages. Green iguanas also enjoy swimming around in a bathtub half-filled with room temperature water!

Keeping Iguanas Safe

Iguanas in the wild face many dangers besides their natural predators. People can destroy or change their habitats. As a result, some kinds of iguanas may soon become **extinct**. For example, over the years, people have brought cats to Jamaica. The cats then hunted iguana eggs and hatchlings. By the 1970s, the Jamaican iguanas were nearly gone.

Many people are trying to save iguanas. Some raise iguanas on farms to eat, rather than hunting them. Zoos raise baby iguanas to put back into the wild. Some countries have passed laws to keep their iguanas safe. If people work together, we can keep the ancient iguana safe for thousands of years to come.

Glossary

ancient (AYN-shent) Very old, from a long time ago.

bask (BASK) To lie in the sun.

burrows (BUR-ohz) Holes an animal digs in the ground to live in.

clutch (KLUCH) The group of eggs laid by a female animal at one time.

equator (ih-KWAY-tur) An imaginary line around Earth that separates it into two parts, northern and southern.

extinct (ek-STINKT) None remaining.

habitats (HA-beh-tats) Kinds of land where animals or plants naturally live.

hatch (HACH) To come out of an egg.

herbivores (ER-buh-vorz) Animals that eat plants.

incubates (IN-kyoo-bayts) Keeps eggs warm.

predators (PREH-duh-terz) Animals that kill other animals for food.

reptile (REP-tyl) A cold-blooded animal with plates called scales.

Index

Web Sites

Due to the changing nature of Internet links, PowerKids Press has developed an online list of Web sites related to the subject of this book. This site is updated regularly. Please use this link to access the list:
www.powerkidslinks.com/scat/iguana/